The Founda

My name is Mark Breitling, a pseudonym borrowed from my favorite watch, not my real name. For years, I've moved in the shadows, navigating a world where truth is often a rare commodity. Lies, deceit, and subterfuge are part of the daily landscape for a spy, and mastering the art of detecting lies is not just a skill—it's a necessity for survival. This book aims to share some of those techniques, giving you the tools to discern truth from falsehood with the precision of a seasoned operative.

Detecting lies is a blend of art and science. It requires keen observation, an understanding of human behavior, and the ability to read subtle cues that most people overlook. The methods I will discuss are grounded in psychological principles, honed through years of experience in the field. They are designed to be practical, applicable in everyday situations, and effective in uncovering the truth.

Understanding the basic nature of deception is crucial. Humans lie for a variety of reasons—fear, gain, protection, or manipulation. The ability to spot these lies can give you a significant advantage in personal and professional settings. But it's not just about catching someone in a lie; it's about understanding the underlying motives and the context in which these lies occur. This deeper comprehension will allow you to navigate interactions more effectively and build stronger, more authentic relationships.

Why do people lie? The reasons are as varied as human nature itself. Some lies are born out of necessity or self-preservation. For example, a person might lie to avoid punishment, embarrassment, or confrontation. These lies often come from a place of fear and are meant to shield the liar from immediate negative consequences. Understanding this motivation can help you empathize with the liar and address the root cause of their deception.

Other lies are told to gain something—be it material benefits, social standing, or personal advantage. These lies are often more calculated and deliberate. A person might exaggerate their accomplishments to seem more impressive, fabricate stories to manipulate others, or withhold critical information to sway a decision in their favor. These lies are typically self-serving and can be more challenging to detect because they are often well-rehearsed and convincingly delivered.

Lies can also be used to protect others. These so-called "white lies" are often told to spare someone's feelings or to avoid causing unnecessary distress. While they might seem harmless, they still represent a departure from the truth and can complicate relationships over time. The intentions behind these lies are usually benign, but they can still have significant consequences if they erode trust.

In some cases, lying becomes a habitual behavior. Chronic liars might lie out of compulsion, even when there is no clear benefit to doing so. This behavior can stem from various psychological issues, including low self-esteem, a need for attention, or an underlying personality disorder. Recognizing habitual lying as a potential sign of deeper issues is essential in understanding and addressing this type of deception.

Context plays a significant role in why people lie. The stakes of a situation often influence the likelihood and nature of deception. In high-stakes environments, such as business negotiations, legal proceedings, or competitive scenarios, the pressure to succeed or avoid failure can lead individuals to lie. In these contexts, lies can be more strategic and calculated, designed to achieve a specific outcome or advantage.

Relationships also heavily influence lying behavior. In personal relationships, lies can be motivated by a desire to maintain harmony, avoid conflict, or protect loved ones. In professional relationships, they might be driven by ambitions, competition, or the desire to maintain a certain image. Understanding the relational dynamics at play can provide valuable insights into why someone might choose to lie in a given situation.

Cultural factors can also influence lying behavior. Different cultures have varying norms and attitudes towards lying and truth-telling. What might be considered a harmless fib in one culture could be seen as a significant breach of trust in another. Being aware of these cultural differences is crucial when interpreting potential deception across diverse interactions.

The impact of lying extends beyond the immediate interaction. Lies can damage trust, create confusion, and lead to unintended consequences. They can strain relationships, erode credibility, and create an environment of suspicion and doubt. Conversely, understanding and effectively dealing with lies can help restore trust, clarify misunderstandings, and foster more transparent and honest communication.

Developing the ability to detect lies is not just about catching someone in the act of deception; it's about fostering a deeper understanding of human behavior and motivation. It's about recognizing the signs that someone is not being entirely truthful and using that knowledge to navigate interactions more effectively. This skill can enhance your personal relationships, improve your professional dealings, and empower you to make more informed decisions.

In the world of espionage, the stakes of detecting lies are often extraordinarily high. Lives can depend on the ability to discern truth from falsehood. While most of us will never face such extreme circumstances, the principles and techniques used by spies can be incredibly valuable in everyday life. Whether you're dealing with a tricky negotiation, a personal conflict, or simply trying to understand someone's true intentions, these skills can give you a significant edge.

What we're exploring here is just the beginning. The world of lie detection is vast and intricate, and this book only scratches the surface. As you practice and refine these techniques, you'll develop a sharper eye for deception and a deeper understanding of human behavior. Welcome to the world of espionage, where the truth is out there if you know where to look.

In the pages that follow, we will delve into specific techniques and real-world examples to help you hone your lie detection skills. From understanding the nuances of human behavior to mastering the art of strategic questioning, you will gain practical tools and insights that can be applied in various aspects of your life. Whether you're navigating professional negotiations, personal relationships, or everyday interactions, these skills will empower you to see through deception and uncover the truth.

The Psychology of Deception

Understanding why people lie is foundational to spotting lies effectively. To truly master the art of deception detection, we must delve deeper into the psychological underpinnings that drive individuals to deviate from the truth. Lying is a universal behavior, but the reasons behind it are as diverse as the people who lie. By exploring these motivations, we can better interpret the signs of deception and navigate the intricate dance of human interaction with greater finesse.

At the heart of many lies is a fundamental drive to protect oneself. Self-preservation lies are often instinctual, triggered by fear of negative consequences. Imagine a child who has broken a vase and lies to avoid punishment. This behavior is not limited to children; adults, too, often lie to escape repercussions. Fear of losing a job, damaging a relationship, or facing legal consequences can prompt even the most honest person to resort to deception.

This protective instinct is closely linked to the concept of loss aversion, a well-documented psychological principle. Humans tend to fear losses more than they value gains of equivalent size. This fear can drive individuals to lie to avoid perceived losses. For instance, an employee might lie about the status of a project to avoid criticism or potential job loss. Understanding this fear-based motivation can help you identify lies that stem from a desire to protect oneself from negative outcomes.

Another common motivation for lying is the pursuit of gain. Lies told for personal gain are often calculated and deliberate. These lies can range from embellishing one's qualifications on a resume to fabricating stories to manipulate others. People lie to gain financial benefits, social status, or competitive advantages. These lies are typically more complex and well-rehearsed, making them harder to detect but often accompanied by subtle clues if you know where to look.

For example, consider someone who exaggerates their achievements to gain admiration and respect. This type of lie is driven by a need for esteem and recognition, reflecting deeper insecurities and desires. Understanding the pursuit of gain as a motivation for lying allows you to look for signs of overcompensation and inconsistency in their stories, which can be indicative of deceit.

Lies can also be altruistic in nature, aimed at protecting others. These "white lies" are often told to spare someone's feelings or prevent unnecessary distress. For instance, telling a friend that their cooking is delicious, even if it isn't, to avoid hurting their feelings. While these lies may seem harmless, they still represent a deviation from the truth and can have significant implications if they become a habitual part of interaction.

In relationships, white lies can be particularly common. People often lie to maintain harmony and avoid conflict. A partner might downplay their frustration to avoid a fight, or a parent might lie to a child to protect them from harsh realities. While the intentions behind these lies are usually benign, they can still erode trust over time if they become pervasive. Recognizing these lies involves understanding the relational dynamics and the desire to preserve peace and stability.

Habitual lying is another fascinating aspect of deception. Some individuals lie out of compulsion, even when there is no clear benefit to doing so. This behavior can stem from various psychological issues, such as low self-esteem, a need for attention, or underlying personality disorders like pathological lying (pseudologia fantastica). Habitual liars often create elaborate, fantastical stories to craft a reality that aligns with their desires and insecurities.

Understanding habitual lying involves recognizing patterns of behavior and inconsistencies over time. Habitual liars often struggle to keep their stories straight, leading to contradictions that can be picked up by a keen observer. These lies are typically more elaborate and may include elements that are easily verified or debunked, providing opportunities for detection.

Cultural influences also play a significant role in lying behavior. Different cultures have varying norms and attitudes towards lying and truth-telling. In some cultures, maintaining harmony and avoiding conflict is highly valued, leading individuals to use more indirect forms of communication, including white lies. In contrast, other cultures may place a higher emphasis on directness and honesty, making lies more noticeable. Understanding these cultural differences is crucial for accurate lie detection across diverse interactions.

For example, in some East Asian cultures, indirect communication and face-saving are important social norms. In these contexts, individuals might use more nuanced and subtle forms of lying to avoid causing embarrassment or discomfort. In contrast, Western cultures, which often value direct communication, might consider these same behaviors as deceitful. Being aware of these cultural norms can help you interpret potential signs of deception more accurately.

The context in which lies occur also significantly influences their nature and detectability. High-stakes environments, such as business negotiations, legal proceedings, or competitive scenarios, often lead to more pronounced signs of deception due to the pressure to succeed or avoid failure. In these settings, the fear of being caught and the potential consequences can heighten stress levels, making it more challenging for liars to maintain their composure.

In professional environments, power dynamics can further complicate lie detection. Subordinates might lie to superiors to avoid negative repercussions or gain favor. These lies can be particularly challenging to detect because the liar is highly motivated to avoid detection and may go to great lengths to maintain their deception. Understanding the power dynamics at play can provide valuable context for interpreting potential signs of lying.

Technological advancements have introduced new dimensions to lying behavior. In today's digital age, lies can be communicated through various mediums, including text messages, emails, and social media. These digital interactions present unique challenges and opportunities for lie detection. For example, written communication lacks the nonverbal cues present in face-to-face interactions, making it more challenging to detect deception. However, analyzing the content, language patterns, and response times in written communication can provide valuable insights into the truthfulness of the message.

Digital deception often involves careful crafting and premeditation, as individuals have more time to think about their responses. This can lead to more polished lies but also opens the door for detailed analysis of the text. For example, inconsistencies in timelines, over-explanation, or a lack of specific details can be indicative of a fabricated story. The absence of typical linguistic markers, such as personal pronouns, can also suggest an attempt to distance oneself from the lie.

Cognitive load plays a critical role in lying behavior. Lying often requires more cognitive effort than telling the truth because the liar must keep track of the false information, maintain consistency, and monitor the other person's reactions. This increased cognitive load can lead to observable signs of stress and difficulty in maintaining the deception. For instance, a liar might exhibit longer response times, increased speech errors, or difficulty maintaining eye contact due to the mental strain of fabricating a story.

Understanding the cognitive aspects of lying involves recognizing the signs of cognitive overload and stress. The concept of cognitive dissonance—the psychological discomfort experienced when holding two or more conflicting beliefs or values—can also come into play. When a person lies, they experience cognitive dissonance between their knowledge of the truth and the false information they are presenting. This dissonance creates internal tension, which can manifest as physical and verbal cues of deception.

Self-awareness and self-regulation are essential skills for effective lie detection. Being aware of your own biases, emotions, and reactions can help you remain objective and focused on the cues and signs that indicate deception. Self-regulation involves maintaining a calm, composed demeanor and avoiding giving away your own thoughts and feelings, which can prevent the liar from gaining an advantage and manipulating your perception.

Building a rapport with the person you suspect of lying can also be a valuable strategy. Establishing a comfortable, non-threatening environment can encourage the liar to lower their guard and become more susceptible to revealing signs of deception. This approach is particularly effective in situations where trust and cooperation are necessary for uncovering the truth.

Understanding the psychology of trust is another crucial aspect of lie detection. Trust is a fundamental component of human relationships, and the violation of trust through lying can have significant emotional and relational consequences. People are generally predisposed to trust others, which can make them more vulnerable to deception. However, once trust is broken, it can be challenging to rebuild. Recognizing the importance of trust and how it influences both lying behavior and the detection process can help you approach lie detection with greater sensitivity and effectiveness.

In addition to understanding individual behavior, it's essential to consider the broader social and environmental context in which lies occur. Environmental factors, such as the setting of the interaction, the presence of others, and the level of privacy, can all influence lying behavior. High-stakes environments, where the consequences of being caught are severe, often lead to more pronounced signs of deception.

However, skilled liars can be adept at masking these signs, making it necessary to look for more subtle cues.

The Impact of technology on lying behavior is also worth considering. In today's digital age, lies can be communicated through various mediums, including text messages, emails, and social media. These digital interactions present unique challenges and opportunities for lie detection. For example, written communication lacks the nonverbal cues present in face-to-face interactions, making it more challenging to detect deception. However, analyzing the content, language patterns, and response times in written communication can provide valuable insights into the truthfulness of the message.

As we delve deeper into these aspects of human behavior, you'll find that detecting lies is not about finding a single "tell" but rather about piecing together a puzzle of behavioral, verbal, and psychological clues. It's about developing a heightened sense of awareness and using this awareness to make informed judgments about the truthfulness of those you interact with.

Remember, what we're exploring here is just the beginning. The world of lie detection is vast and intricate, and this book only scratches the surface. As you practice and refine these techniques, you'll develop a sharper eye for deception and a deeper understanding of human behavior. Welcome to the world of espionage, where the truth is out there if you know where to look.

Strategic Questioning

In the sophisticated dance of lie detection, strategic questioning stands out as a powerful technique. It involves asking carefully crafted questions designed to elicit stress, inconsistencies, or unexpected admissions from the person being questioned. This method requires a blend of psychological insight, observational acuity, and tactical finesse, much like the skillset of a seasoned spy. By mastering strategic questioning, you can uncover hidden truths and detect deception with remarkable accuracy.

Strategic questioning works by exploiting the cognitive load associated with lying. When a person lies, they must juggle multiple tasks simultaneously: fabricating a story, maintaining consistency, monitoring their body language, and gauging your reactions. This mental juggling act increases their cognitive load, making it more challenging to maintain the deception over time. By asking the right questions, you can amplify this cognitive strain, causing cracks to appear in their façade.

To begin with, it's essential to establish a baseline of truthful behavior. Engage the person in casual conversation about neutral topics to observe their normal speech patterns, body language, and reaction times. This baseline will serve as a reference point when you transition to more probing questions. For example, ask them about their favorite hobby or a recent pleasant experience. Notice how they respond, how quickly they answer, and any nonverbal cues they exhibit.

Once you have established a baseline, you can begin to introduce more targeted questions. Open-ended questions are particularly effective because they require the respondent to provide detailed answers, increasing the likelihood of inconsistencies. For instance, instead of asking, "Did you attend the meeting?" you might ask, "Can you walk me through what happened during the meeting?" This forces the person to elaborate, giving you more material to analyze for signs of deception.

As you listen to their response, pay close attention to the level of detail provided. Truthful people tend to give consistent and coherent narratives, while liars often struggle to maintain the same level of detail. They may provide overly elaborate answers to appear convincing or, conversely, be vague to avoid contradicting themselves. Both extremes can be indicative of deceit. Compare their responses to the baseline you established earlier to spot any deviations.

In addition to open-ended questions, the technique of asking unexpected questions can be highly effective. Liars often rehearse their stories to ensure they can deliver a convincing narrative. By asking questions that fall outside the scope of their rehearsed story, you can catch them off guard and increase the chances of eliciting a deceptive response. For example, if someone claims they were at a specific location, ask about minor details that they are unlikely to have prepared for, such as the color of the walls or the background music.

Consider a scenario where an employee is suspected of falsifying their timecard. Instead of directly confronting them with accusations, you could ask, "What did you do after you left the office on the day in question?" If they provide a detailed and plausible story, follow up with a specific question like, "What was the name of the restaurant where you had lunch?" or "Can you describe the route you took home?" These unexpected questions can disrupt their narrative and reveal inconsistencies.

The sequence In which you ask questions can also play a crucial role in strategic questioning. Start with broad, general questions to put the person at ease and then gradually narrow down to more specific, probing inquiries. This gradual progression helps build rapport and makes the person less defensive, increasing the likelihood that they will reveal useful information. Begin with questions like, "Can you tell me about your day yesterday?" and then move to more targeted ones like, "Who did you meet with after lunch?"

Strategic questioning also involves the use of follow-up questions to delve deeper into specific details. When you detect a potential inconsistency or vague response, ask follow-up questions to clarify and probe further. For instance, if someone mentions meeting a friend but provides little detail, you might ask, "What did you and your friend discuss?" or "How long did you spend with your friend?" These follow-up questions can help uncover inconsistencies or additional details that either support or contradict their initial statement.

It's also Important to be mindful of the person's emotional and physiological responses to your questions. Signs of stress, such as increased sweating, fidgeting, or changes in voice pitch, can indicate that they are experiencing cognitive strain. While these signs alone are not definitive proof of lying, they can provide valuable context when combined with other indicators. Observe how their demeanor changes as the questioning progresses and how they respond to different types of questions.

Incorporating silence into your questioning strategy can be a powerful tool. After asking a question, allow a few moments of silence, giving the person time to respond. This can create a sense of discomfort and pressure, especially if they are lying. The discomfort of silence often prompts liars to fill the void with additional details or justifications, increasing the chances of revealing inconsistencies. Use silence strategically to amplify the cognitive load and stress on the liar.

Another technique within strategic questioning is the use of presumptive questions. These are questions that presuppose certain information and can nudge the person into revealing more than they intended. For instance, instead of asking, "Were you at the office all day?" you might ask, "What time did you leave the office?" This presupposes that they left at some point and encourages them to provide details that might not align with their initial story. Presumptive questions can be particularly effective in catching liars off guard.

Consider a situation where you suspect a colleague of misusing company resources. Rather than directly accusing them, you could ask, "When did you first realize you might have exceeded the budget?" This question presupposes that they have exceeded the budget, prompting them to explain their actions. Their response can provide valuable insights into their behavior and intentions, as well as any attempts to cover up their actions.

The art of strategic questioning also involves maintaining a neutral and non-confrontational tone. Accusatory or aggressive questioning can cause the person to become defensive and less likely to provide useful information. Instead, approach the conversation with curiosity and an open mind. This approach helps build rapport and encourages the person to be more forthcoming. For example, use phrases like, "Help me understand..." or "I'm curious about..." to frame your questions in a way that invites cooperation.

To illustrate the power of strategic questioning, consider an interrogation scenario from the world of espionage. A seasoned spy, well-versed in the art of deception, is being questioned about their activities. The interrogator starts with broad questions about the spy's daily routine, establishing a baseline of behavior. Gradually, the questions become more specific, targeting potential weak points in the spy's story. The interrogator uses unexpected questions about minor details, follows up on inconsistencies, and strategically employs silence to increase the cognitive load on the spy. Despite the spy's training, the strategic questioning exposes contradictions and stress indicators, revealing the truth.

In everyday situations, strategic questioning can be just as effective. Whether you're trying to uncover the truth about a friend's suspicious behavior, a partner's evasive answers, or a colleague's questionable actions, the principles of strategic questioning can help you get to the bottom of the matter. By asking the right questions in the right way, you can peel back the layers of deception and reveal the underlying truth.

As you practice and refine your strategic questioning skills, you'll find that this technique becomes a powerful tool in your lie detection arsenal. It requires patience, keen observation, and a deep understanding of human behavior. With time and experience, you'll become adept at crafting questions that cut through the fog of deception and illuminate the truth.

Nonverbal Cues

In the intricate world of lie detection, nonverbal cues play a pivotal role. These subtle signals, often overlooked by the untrained eye, can reveal more about a person's truthfulness than their words ever could. Understanding and interpreting body language, facial expressions, and other nonverbal behaviors are essential skills for anyone aspiring to detect lies with the precision of a seasoned spy. This chapter delves into the art of reading nonverbal cues, providing you with the tools to uncover hidden truths.

Nonverbal communication encompasses a wide range of behaviors, including facial expressions, gestures, posture, eye contact, and even microexpressions. These cues are often subconscious and can provide a window into a person's true feelings and intentions. While words can be carefully chosen and manipulated, nonverbal signals are more difficult to control and therefore more likely to reveal deception.

Let's begin with facial expressions. The human face is incredibly expressive and can convey a vast array of emotions. However, when someone is lying, their facial expressions might not align with their verbal statements. This incongruity is a key indicator of deception. For instance, a person might verbally express happiness while a fleeting microexpression of sadness or fear flashes across their face. These microexpressions are involuntary and last only a fraction of a second, but they can be revealing if you know what to look for.

Microexpressions were popularized by psychologist Paul Ekman, who identified seven universal facial expressions: happiness, sadness, anger, fear, surprise, disgust, and contempt. When people try to mask their true emotions, these microexpressions can leak out, providing crucial clues. For example, if someone claims they are not angry but a brief microexpression of anger appears, it indicates a discrepancy between their words and true feelings. Detecting these subtle cues requires keen observation and practice, but they are invaluable in identifying lies.

Beyond facial expressions, body language offers a wealth of information. Gestures, posture, and movements can all indicate a person's emotional state and truthfulness. When people lie, they often experience a heightened level of stress, which can manifest in various physical ways. Fidgeting, shifting weight, or touching the face are common signs of discomfort that may suggest deceit.

Consider the concept of self-soothing behaviors. These are actions people take to comfort themselves when they are anxious or stressed. For example, touching the face, neck, or hair can be self-soothing behaviors. When someone is lying, they might exhibit these behaviors more frequently as they attempt to manage the stress of deception. Observing an increase in such behaviors during a conversation can be a red flag.

Posture is another critical aspect of body language. A person who is relaxed and confident in their truthfulness will typically have an open and upright posture. In contrast, a person who is lying might display defensive body language, such as crossing their arms, hunching their shoulders, or turning their body away. These defensive postures can indicate discomfort and a desire to shield oneself from scrutiny.

Eye contact is often considered a key indicator of honesty, but it can be a double-edged sword. While it's true that liars might avoid eye contact out of fear of being caught, some skilled deceivers may overcompensate by maintaining intense eye contact to appear more convincing. Therefore, it's essential to consider eye contact in conjunction with other nonverbal cues. A natural, relaxed level of eye contact is generally a good sign, whereas either extreme—too much or too little—can be suspicious.

In addition to these more obvious nonverbal cues, there are other subtle signals to be aware of. The way a person uses their hands can be telling. For instance, when someone is being truthful, their gestures tend to be in sync with their words, reinforcing their message. In contrast, a liar might struggle to coordinate their gestures with their speech, resulting in mismatched or delayed hand movements. This lack of synchronization can be a sign of cognitive overload as the person tries to maintain their lie.

Voice tone and speech patterns also provide valuable insights. Changes in pitch, speed, or volume can indicate stress or anxiety associated with lying. A sudden rise in pitch, for example, might suggest that the person is experiencing tension. Similarly, speaking more quickly or slowly than usual can be a sign of discomfort. Pay attention to these vocal cues and compare them to the person's baseline behavior to spot inconsistencies.

The concept of "leakage" In nonverbal behavior is crucial for lie detection. Leakage occurs when a person's true emotions inadvertently slip out despite their efforts to conceal them. This can happen through microexpressions, body movements, or vocal changes. For example, a person might say they are confident about a decision, but their body language—such as slumped shoulders or averted gaze—leaks their true feelings of doubt or insecurity. Detecting these moments of leakage requires keen observation and an understanding of the interplay between verbal and nonverbal communication.

Context is critical when interpreting nonverbal cues. Different situations and environments can influence how people behave. What might be considered a sign of deception in one context could be perfectly normal in another. For example, someone might avoid eye contact out of cultural norms or personal discomfort rather than deceit. Therefore, it's essential to consider the broader context and baseline behaviors before drawing conclusions about a person's truthfulness.

To illustrate the power of reading nonverbal cues, consider a high-stakes poker game. Experienced players know that their body language can give away their hand, so they work hard to maintain a "poker face." However, even the best players might exhibit subtle tells—unconscious nonverbal signals that reveal their true feelings. A slight twitch, a change in breathing, or an involuntary glance can provide valuable information to a keen observer. Similarly, in everyday interactions, paying attention to these subtle cues can help you detect deception and uncover the truth.

Another real-world example might be a job interview. Interviewers often rely on nonverbal cues to assess a candidate's honesty and confidence. A candidate who maintains open body language, consistent eye contact, and natural gestures is more likely to be perceived as truthful and confident. In contrast, a candidate who exhibits defensive postures, avoids eye contact, or displays incongruent gestures might raise suspicion. By honing your ability to read these nonverbal cues, you can improve your lie detection skills in professional settings.

As you practice and refine your ability to read nonverbal cues, it's essential to develop a holistic approach. Relying on a single cue or sign is rarely sufficient for accurate lie detection. Instead, look for clusters of behaviors that collectively indicate deception. For instance, a combination of fidgeting, inconsistent eye contact, and defensive posture is more compelling evidence of lying than any one of these behaviors alone.

Additionally, self-awareness is crucial. Be mindful of your own body language and how it might influence the person you're observing. Maintaining an open, non-threatening posture and making natural eye contact can help create a comfortable environment, encouraging the other person to relax and reveal more about their true feelings. Your demeanor can significantly impact the interaction and the accuracy of your observations.

Consider practicing your skills in everyday situations. Observe people in various contexts, such as social gatherings, work meetings, or casual conversations. Note their nonverbal behaviors and how they align with their verbal statements. Over time, you'll become more adept at spotting inconsistencies and subtle signs of deception.

To further enhance your skills, study resources on body language and nonverbal communication. Books, courses, and online materials can provide valuable insights and techniques for interpreting nonverbal cues. The more you learn and practice, the sharper your lie detection abilities will become.

Baselining

One of the most powerful techniques for detecting deception is the use of the baseline method. This technique involves observing and establishing a person's normal behavior patterns when they are relaxed and truthful, then comparing these baseline behaviors to how they act when they might be lying. The discrepancies between their baseline and their current behavior can reveal potential deception. Establishing a baseline Is crucial because every individual has unique behavioral traits, and what might be a sign of lying in one person could be perfectly normal in another. This method requires patience, keen observation, and the ability to distinguish between baseline behavior and stress-induced deviations.

To begin with, observe the person in a situation where they are unlikely to be lying. This could be during a casual conversation about a neutral topic or while they are engaged in routine activities. Pay attention to their body language, facial expressions, eye contact, speech patterns, and any idiosyncratic habits they exhibit. Note how they typically respond to questions, how much detail they provide, and how they use gestures to support their speech. This observational period is critical for creating an accurate and comprehensive baseline. The more familiar you become with their normal behaviors, the easier it will be to spot deviations that might indicate lying.

Once you have a solid understanding of their baseline, you can begin to look for changes when the person might be lying. These changes can be subtle or pronounced, depending on the individual's ability to manage stress and conceal their deception. One of the most common indicators of lying is increased nervousness. This can manifest in various ways, such as fidgeting, touching the face, or playing with objects like pens or clothing. While everyone might exhibit some nervous habits, a noticeable increase from their baseline behavior can be a red flag.

Changes in eye contact are also telling. A person who normally maintains steady eye contact might suddenly start looking away more frequently, or vice versa. It's important to note that cultural factors can influence eye contact norms, so consider this in your evaluation. If someone who typically avoids direct eye contact begins staring intensely, or if someone who usually maintains eye contact starts looking around the room, these deviations from their baseline can indicate discomfort or an attempt to manipulate the interaction.

Speech patterns often provide significant clues. Liars may exhibit a variety of changes in their speech, such as hesitations, stammering, or speaking faster or slower than usual. They might also clear their throat more often or take longer pauses before answering questions. Listen for inconsistencies in their story and note any shifts in their tone or pitch. A higher pitch can indicate stress, while a sudden drop in volume might suggest they are trying to hide something. Comparing these vocal changes to their baseline can help you identify potential deceit.

The content of their speech is equally important. Truthful individuals usually provide coherent, detailed, and consistent narratives. In contrast, liars often struggle to maintain the same level of detail and consistency. They might give overly elaborate responses to make their story seem more believable or, conversely, be vague and evasive to avoid getting caught in a lie. Look for discrepancies between their current statements and previous ones, and compare the level of detail they provide to their baseline. Over-explanation or lack of specifics can both be signs of deception.

Physical posture is another area where deviations from the baseline can indicate lying. A person who is normally relaxed and open might become tense and closed off when lying. They might cross their arms, turn their body away, or appear stiff and uncomfortable. Conversely, someone who usually has a more guarded posture might overcompensate by appearing overly relaxed or casual. These shifts in body language, compared to their baseline, can provide valuable insights into their truthfulness.

Facial expressions can be particularly revealing. Microexpressions, which are fleeting facial expressions that occur involuntarily, can betray a person's true feelings even when they are trying to hide them. For example, a quick flash of fear or anger might contradict a person's verbal claim of happiness or calmness. Observing these microexpressions requires keen attention to detail and practice, but they can be a powerful tool in detecting deception. Compare these expressions to their usual facial behaviors to identify inconsistencies.

Another aspect to consider is the timing and coordination of verbal and nonverbal behaviors. In truthful individuals, their words and body language tend to align naturally. However, when someone is lying, there might be a noticeable disconnect between what they are saying and how they are acting. For instance, they might nod while saying no, or their gestures might lag behind their speech. These mismatches can indicate that the person is fabricating their story and struggling to keep their actions in sync with their words.

It's Important to remember that detecting deception using the baseline method is not about identifying a single tell-tale sign but rather observing clusters of behaviors that deviate from the baseline. A combination of increased nervousness, changes in eye contact, altered speech patterns, inconsistent stories, and mismatched verbal and nonverbal cues can collectively point to deception. Each of these signs on its own might not be conclusive, but together they can create a compelling case for lying.

Practical application of the baseline method can be seen in various professional fields. In law enforcement, investigators establish a suspect's baseline during initial, non-threatening conversations, then observe for deviations during more critical questioning. In business negotiations, understanding a counterpart's baseline behavior can help identify when they might be withholding information or misrepresenting their position. Even in personal relationships, knowing a partner's or friend's baseline can help you detect when something is amiss.

Developing proficiency in the baseline method requires practice and patience. Start by observing people in low-stakes situations to hone your skills. Pay attention to how their behaviors align with what they are saying and take mental notes of their baseline patterns. Over time, you will become more adept at recognizing deviations and interpreting their significance. It's also beneficial to continuously refine your observational skills and knowledge of nonverbal communication through study and practical experience.

Remember that context is key. Changes in behavior can be influenced by various factors, including stress, illness, or personal issues unrelated to deception. Always consider the broader context and avoid jumping to conclusions based on isolated observations. The baseline method is a powerful tool, but it must be used with care and consideration for the complexity of human behavior.

By mastering the baseline method, you equip yourself with a sophisticated technique for detecting deception. It allows you to go beyond surface-level observations and delve into the subtleties of human behavior, uncovering hidden truths that might otherwise remain concealed. As you refine your skills, you'll find that this method enhances your ability to navigate interactions with greater insight and accuracy, much like a seasoned spy.

Statement Analysis

Understanding the subtleties of deception requires a blend of keen observation and analytical skills, and few techniques are as powerful in this realm as the use of statement analysis. This method focuses on the words people choose when they speak or write, revealing underlying truths and inconsistencies. By closely examining language, you can detect deception even when the individual appears calm and composed. The key lies in understanding the nuances of how people construct their narratives and identifying patterns that suggest dishonesty.

Statement analysis begins with listening carefully to how a person recounts events. Pay attention to the specific words they use, the structure of their sentences, and any shifts in language. Truthful individuals generally provide coherent, detailed, and consistent narratives. In contrast, those who are lying may exhibit linguistic anomalies that betray their deceit. For example, a person telling the truth will often describe events in chronological order, while a liar might jump around in their timeline to avoid revealing inconsistencies.

One of the primary indicators of deception is the use of vague or ambiguous language. When someone is lying, they often avoid providing specific details that could later be challenged. Instead of saying, "I went to the store and bought a gallon of milk," a deceiver might say, "I went out for a bit and got some things." This lack of specificity serves as a protective mechanism, allowing the liar to maintain flexibility in their story. When analyzing statements, look for these generalized descriptions and consider what information might be intentionally omitted.

Another important aspect of statement analysis is the examination of pronouns. Truthful individuals typically use first-person pronouns, such as "I" and "my," when recounting their experiences. This consistent use of personal pronouns indicates ownership of the story. However, liars often distance themselves from their own narrative to reduce their emotional connection to the lie. They might switch to third-person pronouns or use passive language. For instance, instead of saying, "I parked the car," a liar might say, "The car was parked." This subtle shift can indicate an attempt to dissociate from the falsehood.

Changes in verb tense are also telling. Truthful narratives usually stick to a consistent tense, reflecting the actual sequence of events. However, liars might inadvertently switch tenses, revealing a struggle to keep their story straight. For example, a person might start by describing an event in the past tense—"I went to the store"—and then suddenly switch to the present tense—"and then I am buying milk."

These shifts can indicate cognitive strain as the liar tries to fabricate details while keeping track of their deception.

The level of detail provided is another crucial element to consider. Truthful individuals tend to offer a balanced amount of detail, including sensory descriptions and specific information that paints a vivid picture of the event. In contrast, liars might either overload their story with unnecessary details in an attempt to seem convincing or provide very sparse information to avoid being caught in a lie. For example, a truthful account of a trip might include descriptions of the weather, what the person saw, and how they felt, whereas a fabricated story might lack these sensory details or be overly elaborate without relevant context.

When analyzing statements, it's also important to pay attention to what is not said. Omission is a common tactic in deception. Liars often leave out critical pieces of information that could expose their falsehoods. For instance, someone might say, "I was at home all evening," but avoid mentioning that they briefly went out for an errand. By carefully considering what is missing from the narrative, you can identify potential gaps and probe further.

The use of qualifiers and hedge words is another red flag. Words like "basically," "honestly," "to be fair," and "as far as I remember" can signal that the speaker is not entirely confident in their statements or is trying to create a cushion for potential discrepancies. These qualifiers often indicate that the person is aware their story might not hold up under scrutiny and are preemptively attempting to mitigate that risk.

Inconsistencies within the narrative are perhaps the most obvious indicators of deception. These can manifest as contradictions between different parts of the story or discrepancies between the statement and known facts. For example, if someone claims they were alone at home but later mentions a conversation they had with a friend, this inconsistency can reveal the lie. The key is to listen carefully and compare each part of the statement against the rest and against any other available information.

Another useful aspect of statement analysis is the concept of "emotion in the story." When people recount true events, their emotions tend to align with the narrative. They might express appropriate feelings of joy, sadness, anger, or fear corresponding to the events described. In a fabricated story, however, these emotional cues can be mismatched or absent. For instance, someone describing a traumatic event without showing any signs of distress might be fabricating their story. Similarly, if the emotional tone shifts abruptly without a clear reason, it can indicate deception.

In addition to verbal cues, written statements provide another layer for analysis. Handwritten notes, emails, and text messages can all be scrutinized using the principles of statement analysis. Look for changes in handwriting, unusual word choices, or inconsistent phrasing that could signal deceit. For example, an email that starts formally and ends casually might indicate a shift in the writer's focus or intent. Similarly, overuse of formal language or technical jargon can be a way to obscure the truth.

Practicing statement analysis involves honing your ability to listen and read critically. Start by applying these techniques in everyday conversations. Pay attention to how people describe their experiences and look for patterns in their language. Over time, you will become more adept at identifying the subtle cues that indicate deception. It can also be helpful to analyze historical texts, interviews, or legal statements to see how these principles apply in different contexts.

Remember that statement analysis is not about catching someone in a lie based on a single word or phrase. It involves looking at the overall pattern of speech and writing, considering the context, and comparing it to known facts and behaviors. A single inconsistency or vague statement might not be definitive proof of lying, but multiple indicators taken together can provide a compelling case for deception.

To illustrate the effectiveness of statement analysis, consider the example of a police interrogation. Investigators often use this technique to assess the reliability of a suspect's statement. By analyzing the suspect's choice of words, the structure of their narrative, and any inconsistencies, the investigators can determine whether the suspect is likely telling the truth. This method has been instrumental in solving numerous cases by uncovering lies that would otherwise go unnoticed.

In professional settings, statement analysis can be equally valuable. For instance, in a job interview, paying attention to a candidate's language can reveal whether they are being truthful about their qualifications and experience. If a candidate uses vague language or frequently hedges their statements, it might indicate that they are embellishing their resume. Similarly, in business negotiations, analyzing the language used by the other party can provide insights into their true intentions and help you identify potential areas of dishonesty.

Personal relationships can also benefit from the application of statement analysis. By understanding the principles of this technique, you can navigate conversations with greater awareness and sensitivity. This can help you build stronger, more honest relationships by addressing potential issues of trust and communication more effectively. For example, if you notice that a friend frequently uses qualifiers when discussing certain topics, it might prompt a deeper conversation about their feelings and concerns.

Statement analysis is a powerful tool for detecting deception. By examining the language people use when they speak or write, you can uncover hidden truths and inconsistencies that reveal their true intentions. This technique requires practice, patience, and a keen eye for detail, but it offers a reliable way to discern honesty from deceit. Whether used in professional investigations, business dealings, or personal interactions, statement analysis equips you with the skills to see beyond words and uncover the reality beneath the surface.

Leakage

One of the most intriguing and effective techniques in the realm of lie detection is the analysis of nonverbal behaviors, particularly through the concept known as "leakage." Leakage refers to the involuntary and often unconscious physical signs that reveal a person's true emotions and intentions despite their efforts to conceal them. Understanding and identifying these nonverbal cues can provide invaluable insights into whether someone is telling the truth or attempting to deceive.

Leakage occurs because it is incredibly difficult for most people to control their body language completely when they lie. While they might focus on maintaining a calm and composed demeanor with their words, their body can betray them through subtle cues. These cues include facial expressions, gestures, posture, and other physical behaviors that are less easily controlled. By honing your ability to detect these involuntary signs, you can become adept at spotting lies.

Facial expressions are among the most telling forms of leakage. The face is highly expressive and can reveal emotions that a person might not want to disclose. Microexpressions, which are brief, involuntary facial expressions, can be particularly revealing. These expressions occur when someone is trying to conceal an emotion but cannot suppress the facial muscle reactions completely. For instance, a person might flash a quick microexpression of fear or anger when discussing something stressful, even if they are verbally denying any such feelings.

To spot microexpressions, you need to develop keen observational skills. These expressions can last for just a fraction of a second, so they require close attention and practice to identify. Watching videos of people displaying emotions or practicing with a mirror can help you become more familiar with these fleeting signals. When you detect a microexpression that contradicts what the person is saying, it can be a strong indicator that they are not being entirely truthful.

Gestures are another critical aspect of leakage. People often use their hands to communicate and emphasize their words, but when lying, their gestures might not align with their speech. This incongruence can be a sign of deception. For example, someone might nod their head while saying no or make a gesture that seems out of sync with their verbal message. Such mismatches can indicate that the person is fabricating their story and struggling to keep their actions in line with their words.

Posture and body orientation also provide valuable clues. A person who is lying might exhibit signs of discomfort, such as shifting in their seat, crossing their arms, or turning their body away. These defensive postures can suggest that they are feeling threatened or anxious. Conversely, a person who is being truthful is more likely to have an open and relaxed posture. Observing these changes in body language compared to their baseline can help you detect when someone is not being forthright.

Another important nonverbal cue to watch for is changes in breathing. When people lie, they often experience increased stress, which can lead to changes in their breathing patterns. Rapid, shallow breathing or frequent sighing can be indicators of anxiety. Conversely, a sudden pause in breathing can also suggest that the person is trying to control their physiological responses while fabricating a story. Noticing these subtle changes can provide additional evidence of deception.

Eye behavior is frequently mentioned in discussions of lie detection, but it requires careful interpretation. While it's commonly believed that liars avoid eye contact, this is not always the case. Some individuals might maintain too much eye contact in an effort to appear sincere. Instead of focusing solely on eye contact, consider the context and other accompanying behaviors. Rapid blinking, pupil dilation, or darting eyes can indicate nervousness, which might be associated with lying.

The concept of "emotional leakage" extends beyond facial expressions and gestures to include vocal cues. When people lie, their voices can give them away. Listen for changes in pitch, tone, and speech rate. A sudden rise in pitch, a quiver in the voice, or an increase in speech errors such as stammering or filler words can all indicate stress related to deception. These vocal changes often occur because the cognitive load of lying affects a person's ability to control their vocal output.

Understanding the role of context is crucial in interpreting these nonverbal cues accurately. A person might display signs of stress for reasons unrelated to deception, such as personal issues, nervousness about the situation, or cultural differences in communication styles. Therefore, it's essential to consider the broader context of the interaction and use nonverbal cues in conjunction with other indicators of deception, such as inconsistencies in their story or verbal cues.

One effective way to practice and refine your ability to detect leakage is through role-playing exercises. By simulating scenarios where you and a partner take turns telling the truth and lying, you can observe how different nonverbal cues manifest in real-time. This practice can help you become more attuned to the subtle signs of leakage and improve your overall lie detection skills. Additionally, analyzing recorded interviews or interrogations can provide valuable insights into how nonverbal cues correlate with deception.

Another useful strategy is to combine nonverbal analysis with strategic questioning. By asking open-ended questions and observing the nonverbal responses, you can increase the cognitive load on the person, making it more difficult for them to maintain their deception. For example, if someone claims they were at a particular location, asking them to describe specific details about the environment or their actions can cause stress and reveal inconsistencies through their body language and vocal cues.

In professional settings, the ability to detect leakage can be particularly valuable. For instance, in job interviews, paying attention to a candidate's nonverbal behavior can help you determine whether they are being truthful about their qualifications and experience. Similarly, in negotiations, observing the other party's body language and vocal cues can provide insights into their true intentions and whether they might be withholding information.

Personal relationships can also benefit from an understanding of leakage. By recognizing the signs of deception in everyday interactions, you can address potential issues of trust and communication more effectively. This awareness can help you navigate conversations with greater sensitivity and build stronger, more honest relationships.

Clusters

One of the most advanced and intriguing techniques for detecting deception involves the analysis of behavioral clusters. This method goes beyond looking for individual signs of lying and focuses on identifying patterns of behavior that, when combined, strongly indicate deception. Behavioral clusters are groups of nonverbal and verbal cues that occur together and reinforce each other, providing a more reliable basis for detecting lies. This comprehensive approach requires a deep understanding of human behavior, keen observation skills, and the ability to interpret multiple signals simultaneously.

The foundation of analyzing behavioral clusters lies in the recognition that no single behavior definitively indicates lying. Instead, clusters of behaviors—combinations of gestures, facial expressions, vocal changes, and speech patterns—collectively point to deception. By focusing on these clusters, you can reduce the likelihood of false positives and increase the accuracy of your lie detection.

Begin by establishing a baseline of the person's normal behavior. This step is crucial for understanding their unique patterns of speech and body language when they are relaxed and truthful. Engage them in casual conversation about neutral topics to observe how they typically respond. Note their usual eye contact, gestures, posture, vocal tone, and speech rate. This baseline serves as a reference point for identifying deviations that may indicate lying.

Once you have established a baseline, pay attention to changes in their behavior during more critical or high-stakes conversations. Look for clusters of behaviors that deviate from their norm. For example, a liar might exhibit a combination of increased fidgeting, avoiding eye contact, and a higher-pitched voice when responding to a difficult question. Each of these behaviors alone might not be conclusive, but together they form a cluster that suggests deception.

One common behavioral cluster associated with lying includes physical signs of stress. When people lie, they often experience increased anxiety, which can manifest through various nonverbal cues. For instance, a person might start rubbing their neck, crossing their arms, and tapping their foot. These stress-related behaviors, when observed together, can indicate that the person is uncomfortable and possibly deceptive.

Another cluster involves changes in vocal patterns. Liars often exhibit vocal tension, a higher pitch, and increased use of filler words like "um" and "uh." They might also stammer or take longer pauses before answering questions. Observing these vocal changes in conjunction with other behaviors, such as nervous gestures or inconsistent eye contact, strengthens the case for detecting deceit.

Microexpressions are another critical component of behavioral clusters. These fleeting facial expressions can reveal a person's true emotions, even when they are trying to hide them. For example, a person might briefly display a look of fear or anger before quickly reverting to a neutral expression. When combined with other signs, such as a trembling voice or evasive language, these microexpressions can provide powerful evidence of lying.

Inconsistencies in the narrative form another essential cluster. A liar's story often contains contradictions or lacks coherence. Pay close attention to how the person's account changes over time. For instance, if they initially provide a detailed description of an event but later struggle to recall specific details or change key elements of their story, these inconsistencies can indicate deception. When these narrative inconsistencies occur alongside nervous body language and vocal stress, the overall cluster strongly suggests lying.

Another behavioral cluster involves defensive body language. Liars often adopt a closed-off posture to protect themselves from scrutiny. This can include crossing their arms, turning their body away, or placing objects like a bag or a book between themselves and the questioner. These defensive behaviors, coupled with a reluctance to engage in direct eye contact and a tendency to fidget, form a robust cluster indicating discomfort and potential deceit.

The timing of behaviors is also significant in analyzing clusters. When people lie, their verbal and nonverbal cues often do not synchronize naturally. For example, a person might nod their head while saying no or exhibit a delayed gesture that does not match their spoken words. These mismatches in timing can indicate that the person is fabricating their story and struggling to keep their actions in sync with their lies. Observing these timing discrepancies alongside other signs, like a strained voice or shifting posture, enhances your ability to detect deceit.

Emotional leakage is another aspect of behavioral clusters. When a person lies, their true emotions can slip through despite their efforts to conceal them. This leakage can occur through various channels, such as facial expressions, tone of voice, or body language. For instance, a person might claim to be happy about a decision, but their microexpressions show sadness or anger. When these emotional cues do not align with their verbal statements, it suggests that they are hiding their true feelings and possibly lying.

To effectively use behavioral clusters in lie detection, it is essential to practice and refine your observational skills. Start by paying attention to how people behave in low-stakes situations and note the clusters of behaviors that indicate their comfort and truthfulness. Gradually, apply this knowledge to more critical interactions where the stakes are higher, and the likelihood of deception increases.

Combining behavioral cluster analysis with other techniques, such as strategic questioning and statement analysis, can significantly enhance your lie detection abilities. By creating a multifaceted approach, you increase the cognitive load on the person being questioned, making it more difficult for them to maintain their deception. For example, ask open-ended questions that require detailed responses, then observe the clusters of behaviors that emerge as they answer.

In professional settings, the ability to analyze behavioral clusters can be invaluable. For instance, in law enforcement, investigators use this technique during interrogations to identify when a suspect is lying. They look for clusters of stress-related behaviors, narrative inconsistencies, and defensive body language to determine the truthfulness of the suspect's statements. In business negotiations, understanding the other party's behavioral clusters can provide insights into their true intentions and whether they are being honest about their position.

Personal relationships can also benefit from an understanding of behavioral clusters. By recognizing the signs of deception in everyday interactions, you can address potential issues of trust and communication more effectively. This awareness can help you navigate conversations with greater sensitivity and build stronger, more honest relationships.

The analysis of behavioral clusters is a powerful and advanced technique for detecting deception. By focusing on groups of nonverbal and verbal cues that occur together, you can identify patterns that strongly indicate lying. This method requires keen observation, practice, and the ability to interpret multiple signals simultaneously. Whether used in professional investigations, business dealings, or personal interactions, the ability to detect behavioral clusters equips you with a sophisticated tool to uncover the truth and navigate human interactions with greater insight and accuracy.

Cognitive Loading

One of the more sophisticated and less commonly discussed techniques in lie detection is the use of cognitive load analysis. This method focuses on the mental effort required to construct and maintain a lie, leveraging the fact that lying typically demands more cognitive resources than telling the truth. By increasing the cognitive load on the individual and observing how they respond, you can effectively detect signs of deception.

The premise of cognitive load analysis is straightforward: lying requires a person to fabricate details, keep track of their story, and monitor their behavior to avoid inconsistencies. This added mental effort can lead to observable signs of stress and difficulty, especially when the cognitive demands are intentionally increased during an interrogation or conversation.

To implement this technique, start by creating a baseline of the person's normal cognitive load behavior. Engage them in conversation about neutral topics, asking questions that are straightforward and do not require much mental effort. Observe how they typically respond, noting their speech patterns, eye movements, and body language when they are relaxed and truthful. This baseline will serve as a reference point for detecting changes when cognitive load is increased.

Once you have established a baseline, you can begin to increase the cognitive load by asking more complex and detailed questions. These questions should require the person to think carefully and provide specific information. For example, instead of asking, "Did you go to the store?" ask, "Can you describe everything you did from the moment you left your house until you returned?" This type of question forces the individual to recall and construct a detailed narrative, increasing their cognitive load.

As the person responds, observe for signs of increased cognitive effort. These signs can include longer response times, increased use of filler words like "um" and "uh," and more frequent pauses. These behaviors indicate that the person is experiencing greater cognitive strain. Compare these responses to the baseline you established earlier to identify significant deviations.

Another way to increase cognitive load is to ask the person to recount their story in reverse order. This technique is particularly effective because it disrupts the natural flow of their fabricated narrative, making it more difficult to maintain consistency. For instance, if someone claims they spent the afternoon at a park, ask them to describe their activities in reverse, starting from the moment they left the park and working backward to when they arrived. Most people find it challenging to recount events in reverse, and liars, who have to juggle their fabricated details, will find it even more difficult.

Observe the person's behavior closely during this exercise. Look for signs of hesitation, increased nervousness, and inconsistencies in their story. If they struggle to maintain coherence or become visibly stressed, these are strong indicators that they are lying. The added cognitive load makes it harder for them to keep track of their false narrative, leading to more noticeable signs of deception.

Cognitive load can also be increased by asking unexpected questions that the person is unlikely to have prepared for. Liars often rehearse their stories to ensure they can deliver a convincing narrative. By introducing questions that fall outside the scope of their rehearsed answers, you can catch them off guard and increase the likelihood of detecting deception. For example, if someone claims they were at a specific location, ask about minor details that they are unlikely to have considered, such as the color of the walls or the layout of the space.

Another aspect of cognitive load analysis involves multitasking. When a person is lying, they are already juggling the mental tasks of maintaining their story and monitoring their behavior. By introducing additional tasks, you can further increase their cognitive load and observe how they handle the added pressure. For instance, ask the person to solve a simple puzzle or perform a mental arithmetic task while continuing to answer your questions. This added complexity can make it more difficult for them to maintain their deception.

During this process, watch for signs of cognitive overload, such as increased errors, slower responses, and visible frustration. These indicators suggest that the person is struggling to manage the multiple demands on their cognitive resources, which can lead to slips and inconsistencies in their story.

In addition to these techniques, consider the emotional and psychological aspects of cognitive load. Lying often involves managing emotions like guilt, fear, and anxiety, which can further tax a person's cognitive resources. By creating a context that heightens these emotions, you can increase the cognitive load and make it more challenging for the person to maintain their lie. For example, introduce subtle reminders of potential consequences or emphasize the importance of honesty to elicit emotional responses that add to the cognitive burden.

In professional settings, cognitive load analysis can be particularly valuable. For instance, in law enforcement interrogations, investigators use this technique to increase the cognitive demands on suspects, making it more difficult for them to maintain their deception. By asking detailed and unexpected questions, requesting that suspects recount events in reverse order, and introducing additional tasks, investigators can effectively detect signs of lying.

In business negotiations, understanding cognitive load can provide insights into the other party's honesty. By asking detailed questions about their position and strategy, you can observe how they handle the increased cognitive demands. Signs of stress and inconsistency can indicate that they are not being entirely truthful about their intentions.

Personal relationships can also benefit from an understanding of cognitive load analysis. By recognizing the signs of cognitive strain and deception in everyday interactions, you can address potential issues of trust and communication more effectively. This awareness can help you navigate conversations with greater sensitivity and build stronger, more honest relationships.

To practice cognitive load analysis, start by incorporating these techniques into everyday conversations. Pay attention to how people respond when asked detailed or unexpected questions, and observe for signs of increased cognitive effort. Over time, you will become more adept at recognizing the indicators of cognitive strain and deception.

In conclusion, cognitive load analysis is a powerful and sophisticated technique for detecting deception. By focusing on the mental effort required to construct and maintain a lie, and increasing this cognitive load through detailed questions, reverse-order recounting, and multitasking, you can uncover signs of stress and inconsistency that indicate deceit. This method requires keen observation, practice, and an understanding of human psychology, but it offers a reliable way to discern truth from falsehood. Whether used in professional investigations, business negotiations, or personal interactions, cognitive load analysis equips you with the tools to uncover the truth and navigate human interactions with greater insight and accuracy.

Closing

As we bring this exploration into the art of lie detection to a close, it's essential to recognize that mastering these techniques requires more than just knowledge—it demands practice, keen observation, and a nuanced understanding of human behavior. Throughout this journey, we have delved into various methods, from analyzing nonverbal cues and microexpressions to leveraging cognitive load and linguistic text analysis. Each technique offers unique insights, but together, they provide a comprehensive toolkit for uncovering deception.

The world of espionage teaches us that deception is a multifaceted phenomenon. Lies are woven into the fabric of human interaction, driven by a myriad of motivations and fears. Whether in high-stakes interrogations, business negotiations, or personal relationships, the ability to detect deception can give you a significant edge. It allows you to navigate interactions with greater confidence, discern hidden motives, and make more informed decisions.

Remember, no single indicator is conclusive on its own. The key lies in identifying clusters of behaviors and patterns that collectively suggest deception. It's about piecing together the puzzle of human behavior, using every tool at your disposal to see beyond the surface. This holistic approach ensures that you are not swayed by isolated signs but are instead guided by a broader understanding of the person's actions and words.

Practice is paramount. Start by applying these techniques in everyday situations, honing your skills through continuous observation and analysis. Over time, you will become more attuned to the subtleties of human behavior and more adept at identifying the signs of deception. The more you practice, the sharper your instincts will become, allowing you to detect lies with greater accuracy and confidence.

Ethical considerations are equally important. The power to detect deception comes with a responsibility to use it wisely and compassionately. Remember that the goal is not to catch people in lies for the sake of it but to foster honesty, trust, and transparency in your interactions. Use these skills to build stronger, more authentic relationships, and to navigate the complexities of human behavior with empathy and respect.

As we conclude, reflect on the insights and skills you have gained. Embrace the journey of continuous learning and improvement, knowing that the art of lie detection is both a science and an art. It requires a balance of analytical thinking and intuitive understanding, a blend of observation and empathy. Welcome to the world of the super spy, where every gesture, word, and expression holds the potential to reveal the truth.

Equip yourself with these techniques, practice them diligently, and approach every interaction with a critical yet compassionate eye. In doing so, you will not only become a master of detecting deception but also a more perceptive and understanding observer of human nature. The truth is out there, hidden in plain sight—waiting for those with the skill and patience to uncover it.

Printed in Great Britain
by Amazon